NATIONAL GEOGRAPHIC
School Publishing

Color and Size

Mary Garcia

PICTURE CREDITS
Illustrations by Mini Goss (4–5, 14–15).
Cover, Ibis for Kids Australia; 1, 6 (below left & above center), 7 (above left & below left), 8 (all), 10 (all), 12 (above right), 13 (above, left & right), 16 (above left, center left & center right), Lindsay Edwards Photography; 2, 9 (right), David Sanger Photography/Alamy; 6 (above right), 7 (right), 12 (left), 16 (above right), Getty Images; 9 (left), Detail Parenting/Alamy; 11 (left), 13 (center), 16 (below left), oote boe/Alamy; 11 (right), 16 (below right), Thinkstock/Alamy.

Produced through the worldwide resources of the National Geographic Society, John M. Fahey, Jr., President and Chief Executive Officer; Gilbert M. Grosvenor, Chairman of the Board; Nina D. Hoffman, Executive Vice President and President, Books and Education Publishing Group.

PREPARED BY NATIONAL GEOGRAPHIC SCHOOL PUBLISHING
Ericka Markman, Senior Vice President and President Children's Books and Education Publishing Group; Steve Mico, Senior Vice President and Publisher; Marianne Hiland, Editorial Director; Lynnette Brent, Executive Editor; Michael Murphy and Barbara Wood, Senior Editors; Bea Jackson, Design Director; David Dumo, Art Director; Margaret Sidlowsky, Illustrations Director; Matt Wascavage, Manager of Publishing Services; Sean Philpotts, Production Manager.

MANUFACTURING AND QUALITY MANAGEMENT
Christopher A. Liedel, Chief Financial Officer; Phillip L. Schlosser, Director; Clifton M. Brown III, Manager.

BOOK DEVELOPMENT
Ibis for Kids Australia Pty Limited.

Copyright © 2006 National Geographic Society. All rights reserved. Reproduction of the whole or any part of the contents without written permission from the publisher is prohibited. National Geographic, National Geographic *Windows on Literacy*, and the Yellow Border are registered trademarks of the National Geographic Society.

Published by the National Geographic Society
1145 17th Street, N.W.
Washington, D.C. 20036-4688

ISBN 0-7922-6052-X

Third Printing 2008
Printed in China

Contents

Think and Discuss	4
Red	6
Blue	8
Yellow	10
Different Colors, Different Sizes	12
Use What You Learned	14
Picture Glossary	16

Think and Discuss

Things are different colors and sizes. What colors and sizes do you see?

Red

Find the red things.

Is the red bear BIG or small?
teddy bears

Blue

Find the blue things.

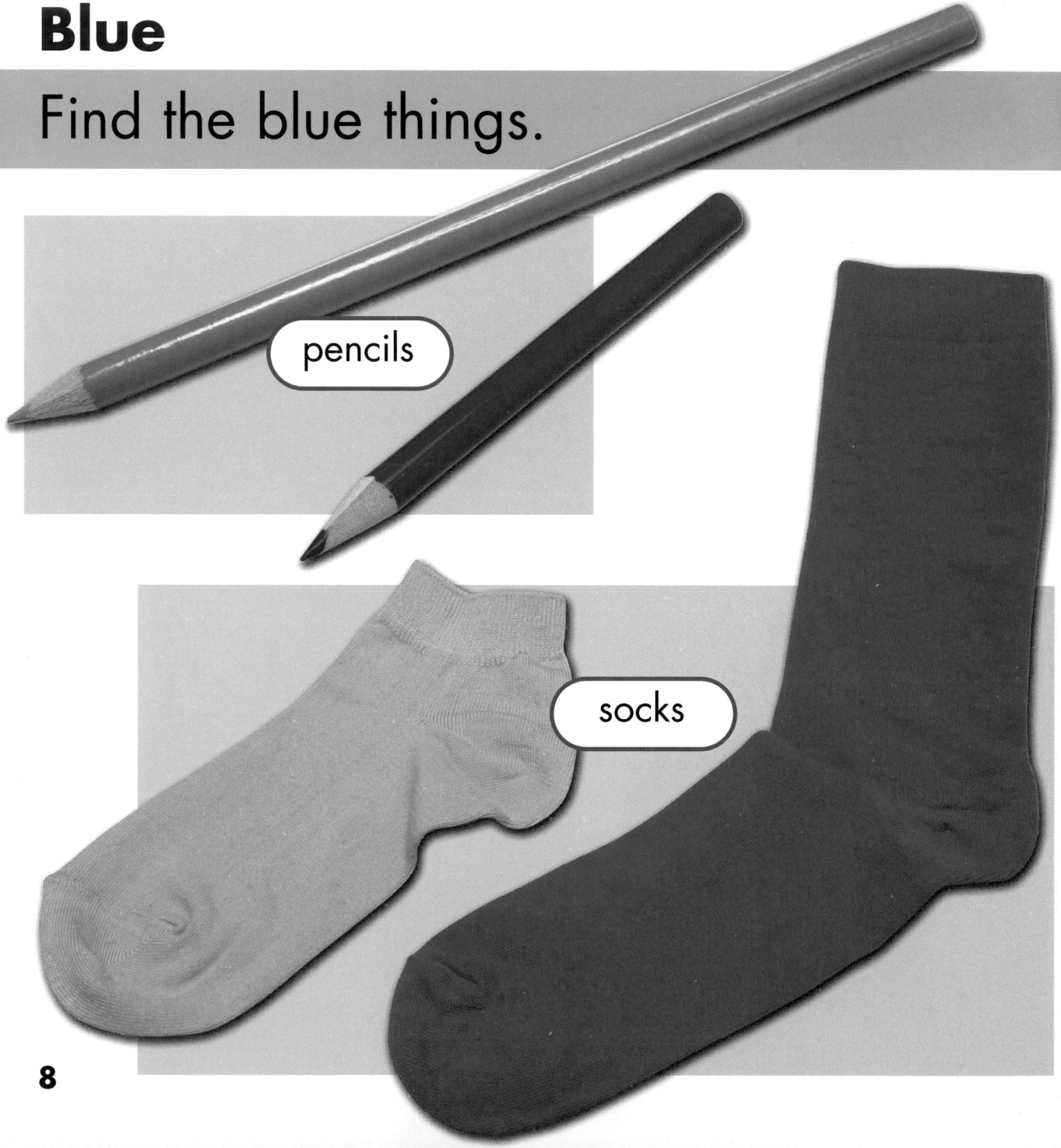

Is the blue slide long or short?
slides

Yellow

Find the yellow things.

Is the yellow ladder tall or short?

ladders

Different Colors, Different Sizes

Things are different colors.
Things are different sizes.

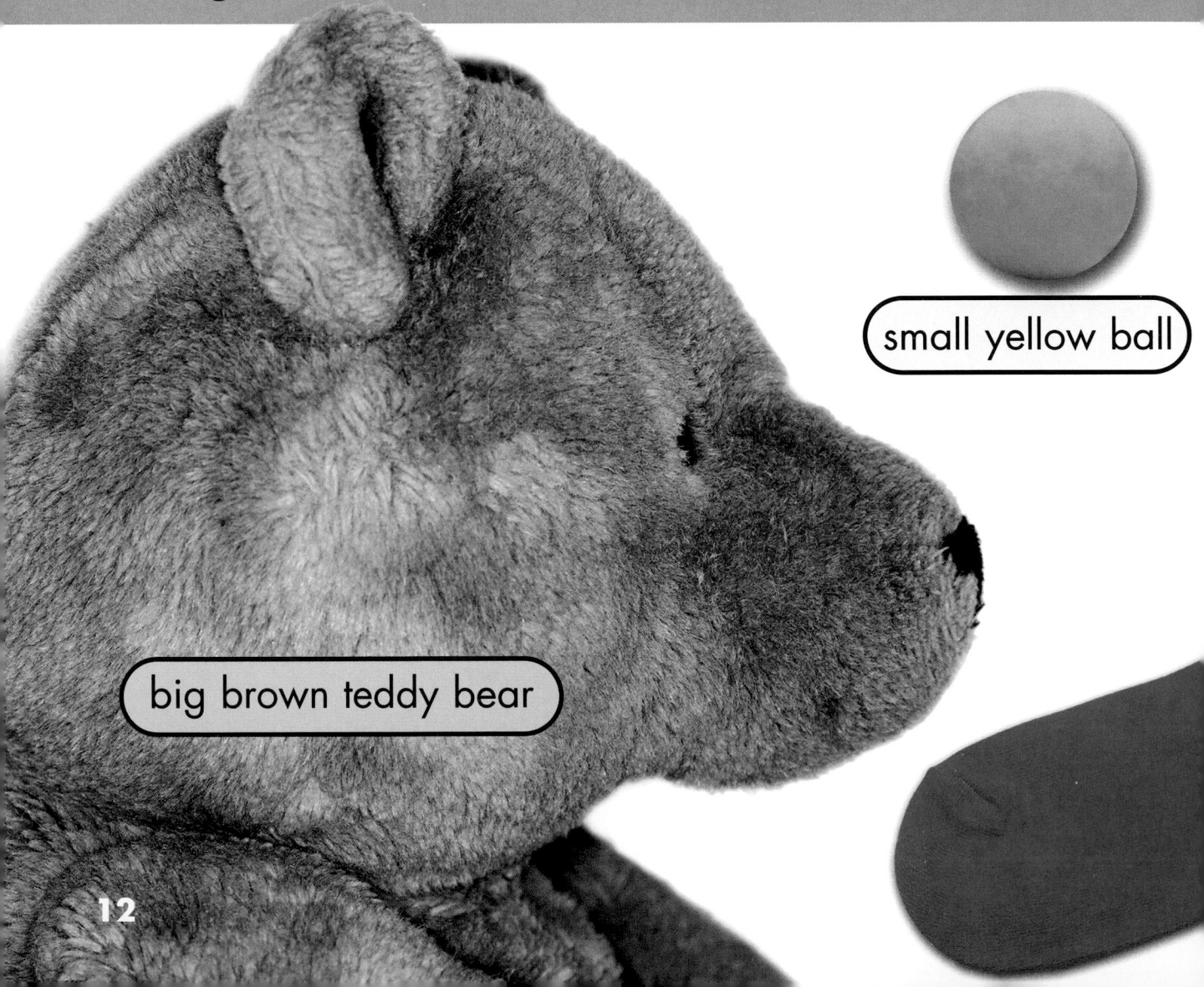

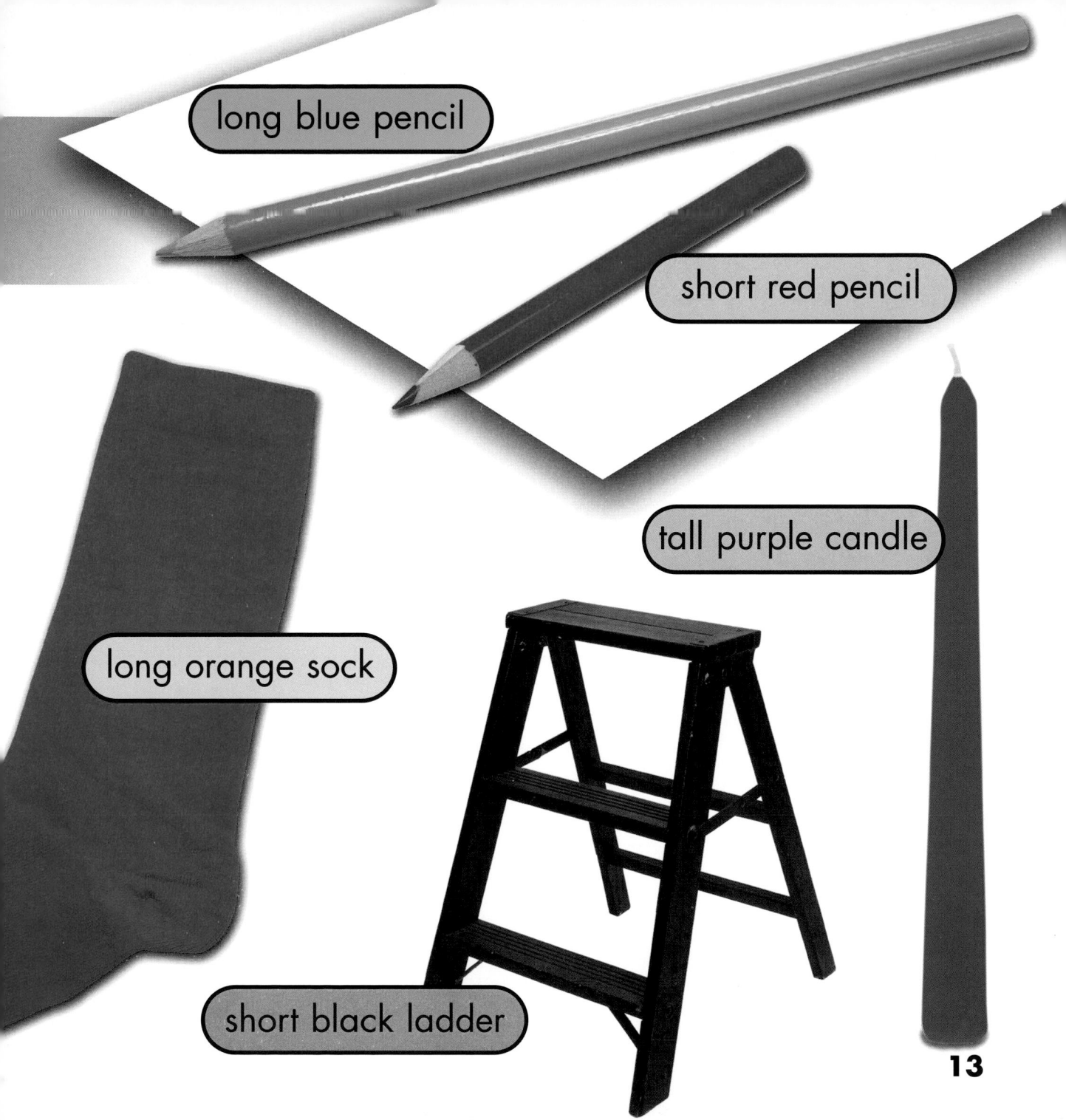
long blue pencil
short red pencil
tall purple candle
long orange sock
short black ladder

Use What You Learned

Things are many different colors and sizes. What different colors and sizes do you see?

COLOR

black
blue
green
orange
purple
red
yellow

SIZE

big
long
short
small
tall

Picture Glossary

black

blue

green

orange

purple

red

yellow

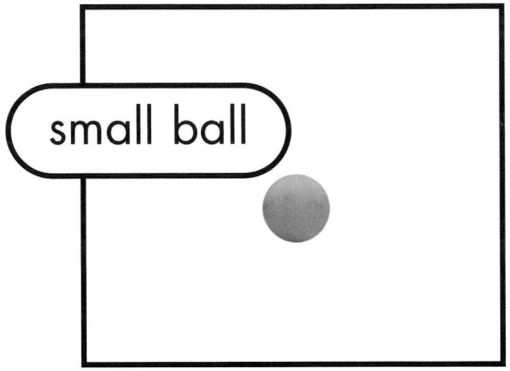

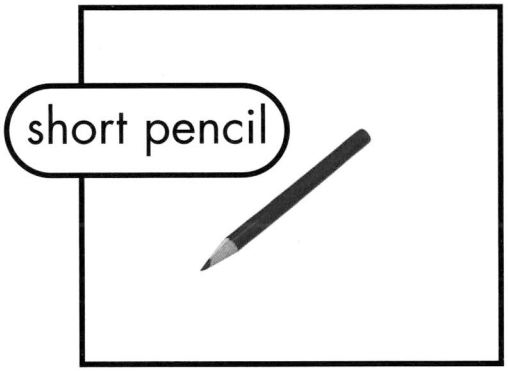

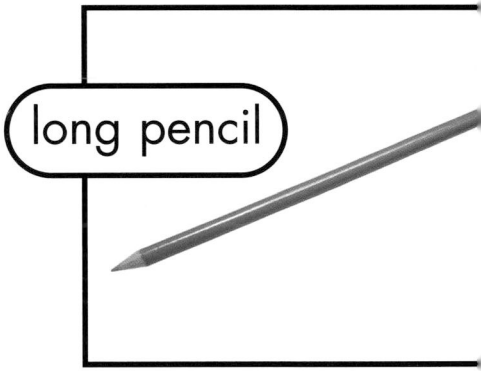